SUBSCRIBE TO PEWDIEPIE

To the king of YouTube, the bearded Hmmmmmmmmer of wonder, reviewer of memes, and his gibbering army of nine year olds.

Say no to T-Series, rustle up a steaming bitch lasagna, and let's make YouTube great again.

I'M DOING MY PART. ARE YOU?

There comes a time in everyone's life when a calling bigger than oneself comes knocking. When one feels a rapid beating of the heart, a passion in the soul, perhaps even a strange and overwhelming stirring in the loins.

When that moment arrives, as it has for you, it is time to stand up and be counted.

A battle is raging, perhaps the battle to end all battles. Will you choose to play your part?

If you've been given this book, then there is a simple reason: you have been chosen to fight.

It is your time to subscribe to PewDiePie.

So, dust off your best pair of trousers, power up your interwebs, and strap yourself in for a big slice of what you're going to do next.

Good luck, soldier. Only the strongest will make it.

Now, get yourself on YouTube, oil-up your clicking finger,

and...

SUBSCRIBE TO PEWDIEPIE

SUBSCRIBE TO PEWDIEPIE

SUBSCRIBE TO PEWDIEPIE

SUBSCRIBE TO PEWDIEPIE

SUBSCRIBE TO PEWDIEPIE

SUBSCRIBE TO PEWDIEPIE

SUBSCRIBE TO PEWDIEPIE

SUBSCRIBE TO PEWDIEPIE

SUBSCRIBE TO PEWDIEPIE

SUBSCRIBE TO PEWDIEPIE

SUBSCRIBE TO PEWDIEPIE

SUBSCRIBE TO PEWDIEPIE

SUBSCRIBE TO PEWDIEPIE

SUBSCRIBE TO PEWDIEPIE

SUBSCRIBE TO PEWDIEPIE

SUBSCRIBE TO PEWDIEPIE

SUBSCRIBE TO PEWDIEPIE

SUBSCRIBE TO PEWDIEPIE

SUBSCRIBE TO PEWDIEPIE

SUBSCRIBE TO PEWDIEPIE

SUBSCRIBE TO PEWDIEPIE

SUBSCRIBE TO PEWDIEPIE

SUBSCRIBE TO PEWDIEPIE

SUBSCRIBE TO PEWDIEPIE

SUBSCRIBE TO PEWDIEPIE

SUBSCRIBE TO PEWDIEPIE

SUBSCRIBE TO PEWDIEPIE

SUBSCRIBE TO PEWDIEPIE

SUBSCRIBE TO PEWDIEPIE

SUBSCRIBE TO PEWDIEPIE

SUBSCRIBE TO PEWDIEPIE

SUBSCRIBE TO PEWDIEPIE

SUBSCRIBE TO PEWDIEPIE

SUBSCRIBE TO PEWDIEPIE

SUBSCRIBE TO PEWDIEPIE

SUBSCRIBE TO PEWDIEPIE

SUBSCRIBE TO PEWDIEPIE

SUBSCRIBE TO PEWDIEPIE

SUBSCRIBE TO PEWDIEPIE

SUBSCRIBE TO PEWDIEPIE

SUBSCRIBE TO PEWDIEPIE

SUBSCRIBE TO PEWDIEPIE

SUBSCRIBE TO PEWDIEPIE

SUBSCRIBE TO PEWDIEPIE

SUBSCRIBE TO PEWDIEPIE

SUBSCRIBE TO PEWDIEPIE

SUBSCRIBE TO PEWDIEPIE

SUBSCRIBE TO PEWDIEPIE

SUBSCRIBE TO PEWDIEPIE

SUBSCRIBE TO PEWDIEPIE

SUBSCRIBE TO PEWDIEPIE

SUBSCRIBE TO PEWDIEPIE

SUBSCRIBE TO PEWDIEPIE

SUBSCRIBE TO PEWDIEPIE

SUBSCRIBE TO PEWDIEPIE

SUBSCRIBE TO PEWDIEPIE

SUBSCRIBE TO PEWDIEPIE

SUBSCRIBE TO PEWDIEPIE

SUBSCRIBE TO PEWDIEPIE

SUBSCRIBE TO PEWDIEPIE

SUBSCRIBE TO PEWDIEPIE

SUBSCRIBE TO PEWDIEPIE

SUBSCRIBE TO PEWDIEPIE

SUBSCRIBE TO PEWDIEPIE

SUBSCRIBE TO PEWDIEPIE

SUBSCRIBE TO PEWDIEPIE

SUBSCRIBE TO PEWDIEPIE

SUBSCRIBE TO PEWDIEPIE

SUBSCRIBE TO PEWDIEPIE

SUBSCRIBE TO PEWDIEPIE

SUBSCRIBE TO PEWDIEPIE

SUBSCRIBE TO PEWDIEPIE

SUBSCRIBE TO PEWDIEPIE

SUBSCRIBE TO PEWDIEPIE

SUBSCRIBE TO PEWDIEPIE

SUBSCRIBE TO PEWDIEPIE

SUBSCRIBE TO PEWDIEPIE

SUBSCRIBE TO PEWDIEPIE

SUBSCRIBE TO PEWDIEPIE

SUBSCRIBE TO PEWDIEPIE

SUBSCRIBE TO PEWDIEPIE

SUBSCRIBE TO PEWDIEPIE

SUBSCRIBE TO PEWDIEPIE

SUBSCRIBE TO PEWDIEPIE

SUBSCRIBE TO PEWDIEPIE

SUBSCRIBE TO PEWDIEPIE

SUBSCRIBE TO PEWDIEPIE

SUBSCRIBE TO PEWDIEPIE

SUBSCRIBE TO PEWDIEPIE

SUBSCRIBE TO PEWDIEPIE

SUBSCRIBE TO PEWDIEPIE

SUBSCRIBE TO PEWDIEPIE

SUBSCRIBE TO PEWDIEPIE

SUBSCRIBE TO PEWDIEPIE

SUBSCRIBE TO PEWDIEPIE

SUBSCRIBE TO PEWDIEPIE

SUBSCRIBE TO PEWDIEPIE

SUBSCRIBE TO PEWDIEPIE

SUBSCRIBE TO PEWDIEPIE

SUBSCRIBE TO PEWDIEPIE

SUBSCRIBE TO PEWDIEPIE

SUBSCRIBE TO PEWDIEPIE

SUBSCRIBE TO PEWDIEPIE

SUBSCRIBE TO PEWDIEPIE

SUBSCRIBE TO PEWDIEPIE

SUBSCRIBE TO PEWDIEPIE

SUBSCRIBE TO PEWDIEPIE

SUBSCRIBE TO PEWDIEPIE

SUBSCRIBE TO PEWDIEPIE

SUBSCRIBE TO PEWDIEPIE

SUBSCRIBE TO PEWDIEPIE

SUBSCRIBE TO PEWDIEPIE

SUBSCRIBE TO PEWDIEPIE

SUBSCRIBE TO PEWDIEPIE

SUBSCRIBE TO PEWDIEPIE

SUBSCRIBE TO PEWDIEPIE

SUBSCRIBE TO PEWDIEPIE

SUBSCRIBE TO PEWDIEPIE

SUBSCRIBE TO PEWDIEPIE

SUBSCRIBE TO PEWDIEPIE

SUBSCRIBE TO PEWDIEPIE

SUBSCRIBE TO PEWDIEPIE

SUBSCRIBE TO PEWDIEPIE

SUBSCRIBE TO PEWDIEPIE

SUBSCRIBE TO PEWDIEPIE

SUBSCRIBE TO PEWDIEPIE

SUBSCRIBE TO PEWDIEPIE

SUBSCRIBE TO PEWDIEPIE

SUBSCRIBE TO PEWDIEPIE

SUBSCRIBE TO PEWDIEPIE

SUBSCRIBE TO PEWDIEPIE

SUBSCRIBE TO PEWDIEPIE

SUBSCRIBE TO PEWDIEPIE

SUBSCRIBE TO PEWDIEPIE

SUBSCRIBE TO PEWDIEPIE

SUBSCRIBE TO PEWDIEPIE

SUBSCRIBE TO PEWDIEPIE

SUBSCRIBE TO PEWDIEPIE

SUBSCRIBE TO PEWDIEPIE

SUBSCRIBE TO PEWDIEPIE

SUBSCRIBE TO PEWDIEPIE

SUBSCRIBE TO PEWDIEPIE

SUBSCRIBE TO PEWDIEPIE

SUBSCRIBE TO PEWDIEPIE

DO IT NOW.

WWW.YOUTUBE.COM/USER/PEWDIEPIE

Printed in Great Britain
by Amazon